Wedding Speeches
& Toasts

Wedding Speeches
& Toasts

Carole Hamilton

RYLAND
PETERS
& SMALL

LONDON NEW YORK

Senior Designer Liz Sephton
Senior Editors Miriam Hyslop and Catherine Osborne
Picture Researcher Emily Westlake
Production Gemma Moules
Publishing Director Alison Starling

First published in 2007
in the United States by
Ryland Peters & Small, Inc.
519 Broadway
5th Floor
New York, NY 10012
www.rylandpeters.com

Text, design, and photographs
© Ryland Peters & Small 2007
10 9 8 7 6 5 4 3 2 1

Printed and bound in China

ISBN-10: 1-84597-504-9
ISBN-13: 978-1-84597-504-3

contents

introduction

Making any kind of speech is daunting, but somehow it's even more nerve-racking when the speech is for a wedding, because you are expected to add something meaningful to such a special occasion.

If you've been asked to speak at a wedding —which presumably you have, otherwise you wouldn't be nervously flicking through this book—you are probably experiencing some mixed emotions. On the one hand, it's an honor to be asked. Someone thinks enough of you to want you to stand up and utter some words of wisdom at their wedding. On the other hand, a feeling of dread has already filled your stomach, even though the wedding is still months away!

Try not to worry too much, though. Otherwise, you run the risk of not enjoying the big day, which would be a shame. The pressure you are feeling is mostly self-inflicted and nobody else will expect a perfect performance. You will be speaking to friends and family and, providing your words come from the heart, you can't really go wrong.

So, whether you are the bride, the groom, father of the bride, or the best man, use this book for inspiration as well as preparation for your moment in the spotlight. You will find hints and tips on everything you need to know, plus a host of quotable quotes and meaningful toasts.

Nothing can guarantee a completely stress-free speech, but if you're well prepared and well rehearsed, I have a sneaking feeling you may even enjoy it!

Carole Hamilton

GETTING STARTED

unaccustomed as I am ...

Standing up and speaking in front of a room full of people, even when they are family and friends, is nerve-racking. All but the most confident person is going to feel the odd twinge of panic that what they are about to say will fall flat and be greeted by silence rather than applause.

The secret to successful speaking, whether you've been asked to propose a toast or give a full-blown speech, is preparation. If you know what you're going to say and have practiced beforehand, you're going to feel more confident and less nervous when it comes to the big day. The most important thing to remember is that you are speaking to friends, and the only pressure you're under is the pressure you put on yourself. Nobody else expects an Oscar-winning performance. Providing your words are heartfelt and sincere, with the odd line that makes your audience smile, you'll have achieved your objective.

It usually takes me more than three weeks to prepare a good impromptu speech.
Mark Twain (1835–1910)

Any nerves will kick in on the wedding morning, and having something to eat will go a long way to calming a queasy stomach. Even if you don't feel hungry, it's a good idea to eat a bagel or some cereal. Try to avoid coffee and tea, which will give you an instant buzz then a "caffeine slump" just in time for your speech. Alcohol is also best avoided until after your starring moment. One glass will probably take the edge off the panic, but any more and you could be in danger of slurring your words or becoming over-confident and adding something that was best left at home! While there's lots you can do to help calm last-minute jitters, you shouldn't want to banish them altogether—a little adrenaline has helped many a great performance.

- Do have something to eat on the wedding morning. It will calm the butterflies in your stomach.

- Don't write down every word. Cue cards are more effective and will help your words sound more spontaneous.

- Do practice what you intend to say, asking a friend to listen to make sure you're speaking clearly and can be heard across a good-sized room.

- Don't forget to look up when you're speaking. Focus on something toward the back of the room—and remember to smile.

- Do remember that your audience is not there to criticize. Most of them are just thankful it's not them up there speaking!

- Don't forget to speak slowly. Many a great speech was ruined because the speaker rushed through it so fast, jokes were missed and subtleties lost.

planning and preparation

Nerves are generally caused by the fear of the unknown, so preparing your speech well in advance will go a long way to quelling any apprehension you may have.

Before you think about the content of your speech, ask yourself what other people are expecting to hear. Aside from the traditional thanks and good wishes, what else will you bring to the occasion? Are you renowned for being old and wise, for being a long-standing friend of the family, and therefore having lots of stories to tell, or are you well known for being confident and great at telling jokes?

It is important to remember that your speech needs to be about the wedding and your relationship with the bride and groom. It is not a vehicle for self-promotion. The next thing you need to do is some research, so that your speech will feel personal to both the bride and the groom.

Start with the family of the bride and groom—not just parents and siblings, but grandparents and aunts and uncles too. Find out as much as you can about each family. How long have they lived in the area? How long have parents/grandparents been married? Are any family members well known? Do they have any stories to tell about the bride or groom when they were growing up?

Once you've exhausted family contacts, move on to old school and college friends as well as past and present work colleagues. The more people you talk to, the more information you will gather to form the basis of your speech. Even if you are the groom, there are bound to be things you didn't know about your bride, so give yourself plenty of time to do lots of research.

Write down everything you've been told by family and friends and you should see the basis of your speech coming together. It won't be necessary to include details from every story, as some things may just warrant a general mention, but chances are you will have discovered some great anecdotes that will delight and even surprise many of the wedding guests. Just don't pick anything too risqué!

writing your speech

Once you have collated your background material, you'll want to stop thinking and start writing. Don't expect your first draft to be perfect. Your speech is likely to be fine-tuned many times during the preparation process, but getting your first thoughts down on paper will give you a real confidence boost.

Any speech needs a start, a middle, and an end, and it's usually best to write your thoughts in this order to avoid forgetting anything important. Make rough notes to start with, rather than trying to write complete sentences.

To avoid any awkward pauses, each section of your speech needs to flow into what follows. Think about using some link phrases like "which leads me nicely on to …" rather than finishing one story and abruptly starting another.

Try to write the way you speak. This is often quite different to the language you use in a document which is meant to be read rather than spoken aloud. Avoid using too many colloquialisms or double-entendres that are easily lost in translation—particularly if any of your audience is old or do not speak English as a first language.

Once you are happy with your first draft, put it away and forget about it for a few days. The second reading is the time to ask yourself some searching questions about the content:

🐝 Is it too short or too long?

🐝 Does it suit the overall tone and formality of the wedding?

🐝 Is there anything that may offend even one of the guests?

🐝 Are the jokes actually funny?

🐝 Does it flow smoothly? Have you repeated any words or phrases?

🐝 Does it tick all the boxes of who needs to be thanked?

Finally, ask a trusted friend to listen as you give your speech. Then get them to give you an honest opinion about the content and the delivery.

pace, timing, and length

The ideal length of your speech largely depends on your role and the formality of the wedding. The father of the bride, the bride, and the groom tend to give shorter speeches than the best man. Traditionally, the more formal the wedding, the shorter (and less joke-filled) the speeches will be.

Whoever you are, you should be aiming to speak for between five and ten minutes. If that doesn't sound very long, try timing yourself as you read a section from a newspaper. It's probably a lot more words than you imagined. But be warned: if your speech is too long, you risk losing the attention of your audience. It's better to leave them wanting more than wishing you would just shut up!

Practice makes perfect and it's important that you rehearse reading your speech aloud. This not only helps you to familiarize yourself with the content, but it will do wonders for your confidence. Ideally you should practice reading in front of other people and, if at all possible, in a large room that is about the size of the reception hall.

Aim to speak slowly and clearly, pausing at the end of sentences and after any jokes to allow room for laughter. Many inexperienced speakers speak too quickly, which means their audience is likely to miss the subtleties they've worked so hard to include. If you feel yourself getting flustered, stop for a minute and take a sip of water. A little break will get you back on track.

The best way to make a good speech is to have a good beginning and a good ending and have them close together.
Anonymous

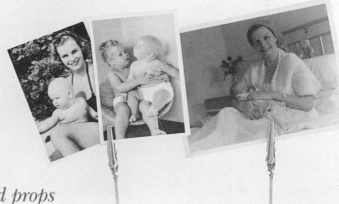

humor and props

Humor is an essential part of just about any speech, but you need to work at getting the balance right. Remember that the main purpose of any speech is to celebrate the marriage of two people, and not to prove that you've missed your vocation as a stand-up comic.

When thinking about which jokes to include in your speech, consider long and hard who is in the audience. The style of humor that will appeal to younger friends is quite likely to offend some of the older guests. Steer clear of anything overtly sexual and anything to do with religion or politics. And it's probably best not to swear, particularly if there will be children in attendance.

For inspiration, look in reference books and on the internet for humorous quotations about love and marriage. You will also find lots of funny one-liners suited to weddings, which can be dropped in at an appropriate moment to add emphasis or to introduce one of your own stories.

Props can also be a useful part of a speech, especially the best man's speech, when everyone is expecting to be entertained. Some speakers have even gone as far as preparing a video of "on camera" anecdotes from friends and family or compiling themed boards of photographs charting the bride and groom through childhood, adolescence, and during their relationship. This obviously takes a lot of planning, but if you are confident about the content and your ability to deliver it well, it will make for a memorable performance.

Every mother generally hopes that her daughter will snag a better husband than she managed to do … but she's certain that her boy will never get as great a wife as his father did.

Anonymous

delivering your speech

Once you are happy with the content of your speech, you will need to think about the delivery. Trying to commit the whole thing to memory isn't a good idea. You are bound to forget something, which will instantly leave you feeling flustered and undermine your confidence. Reading the whole speech out, word for word, is also a recipe for stilted delivery.

Your best bet is to use prompt cards. This is what all professional speakers use and involves putting key names, dates and phrases onto a series of small reference cards. Every time you change the subject, use a new cue card. Write in black ink and number each card. That way, you can be sure they are kept in the right order.

Once you have familiarized yourself with what you want to say, the cards will be all you need to recount a story or tell a joke. Many people imagine that they will forget what to say, but you won't, and the delivery will sound much more relaxed and engaging to your audience.

Prompt cards also allow you to look up at your audience rather than looking down, as you would if you read a speech word for word. So your voice projects out across the audience, focus on something such as a picture toward the back of the room. If people look like they are straining to hear you, speak up.

If you are speaking at a very large wedding, you may be offered a microphone. They can be very useful, but take a minute to practice before the reception starts. Then you will know how loud to make your voice—you don't want to startle everyone as you start to speak!

Speak clearly, if you speak at all; carve every word before you let it fall.
Oliver Wendell Holmes 1809–1894

SPEECHES

*There is only one happiness in life, to love
and be loved.*
George Sand (1804–1876)

speech and toast etiquette

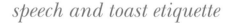

Speeches and toasts are an integral part
of any wedding. They tend to follow after
the meal but before the cake-cutting
ceremony in a pretty standard order.

At the most formal style of wedding, a
toastmaster will introduce the father of
the bride once the guests have finished
eating and coffee has been served. If
there isn't a toastmaster, the best man will
usually get up and attract the attention of
the audience by tapping a glass to indicate
the speeches are about to begin.

The father of the bride is followed
by the groom. If the bride is going
to speak, she can either get up at the
same time as the groom or immediately
afterward. If the maid of honor or either
of the groom's parents want to say a few
words—and increasingly this is the case—
they should speak after the bride and
groom and before the best man. The
best man will then bring the speeches
to a close with a final toast to the bride
and groom, and announce the cutting
of the cake.

Be prepared for the meal, and therefore the speeches, to run late. Also provide chairs for the arrival of any evening-only guests, so they can slip in quietly and sit down without distracting the speaker.

At an informal wedding, or if the thought of the speeches looks likely to ruin the meal for those involved, it is perfectly acceptable to have the speeches before the food is served. Just make sure everyone involved knows the timings and doesn't disappear at an inopportune moment.

If you are making a speech at a second-time round wedding (and about forty percent of weddings involve someone on a second marriage), the speeches and toasts follow much the same format. However, when it comes to making your speech, it's important that you don't dwell on the fact that either or both the bride and groom have been married before. A passing reference to "braving matrimony for a second time" is fine, but details about previous relationship problems are best left unsaid.

pre-wedding speeches

There are a number of occasions before the wedding when you may be called upon to say a few words, and you will want to be prepared for these, as well. Engagement parties and bachelor parties and bridal showers do not involve any formal toasts, but several of the key members of the bridal party are likely to be asked to make a short, impromptu speech. If this could be you and you are not good at thinking on your feet, give it some thought beforehand. Jotting down a few well-chosen words of congratulations will avoid you being struck dumb if the spotlight falls on you unexpectedly. Since many of the same guests will be at the wedding, don't give away any of your best stories, and keep it short and sweet. The bride and groom may also be called upon to "reply" to the simplest words, so need to prepare a light-hearted response.

Sample toast for an engagement party

I am delighted to have been asked to propose a toast to (name of bride and groom) to mark the wonderful occasion of their engagement. I think you will all agree that they make the perfect couple and will you now join me in wishing them a long and very happy life together. Please raise your glasses to (name of bride and groom).

Sample words for a bridal shower/bachelor party

We are here today to help (name of bride/groom) say goodbye to the single life. Try as I might, I have been unable to persuade (her/him) that marriage is not for them. Why does anyone in their right mind want to give up bars/parties/football/shopping and replace it with housework/monogamy/DIY/babies? But the lure of the married life has obviously proved too strong, and next Saturday we will all be there to witness the moment when (name of bride/groom) finally ties the knot. So grab a tissue—sorry, I mean a glass—and join me in wishing her/him the very best of everything. To (name of bride/groom).

the rehearsal dinner

Formal weddings are likely to involve a wedding rehearsal a few days before the actual event, so that all the main bridal party can practice their roles for the big day. All the key players—including the celebrant, the bride, groom, best man, parents, and bridesmaids—meet and rehearse everything that will happen during the ceremony. Once this is over, it is usual for the bride and groom and their parents to host an informal rehearsal dinner, and short speeches are usually part of the evening.

Unlike the wedding reception, this is an occasion when more than just the parents and the best man may like to say a few words of congratulations. And, since it is an informal event, there doesn't need to be a set running order, although any speeches and toasts would normally follow once the meal is over.

The father of the bride usually kicks off the speeches by welcoming and thanking everyone for taking the time to attend the rehearsal. This is also a good opportunity to welcome any out-of-town guests who may have just arrived. The bride and/or groom then offer thanks to one or both sets of parents for hosting such a wonderful evening.

Once this part is over, anyone who wants to say a few words is welcome to do so. If you are not one of the key members of the bridal party or already speaking at the wedding, this is a great opportunity to share a funny or touching story about the couple with their closest family and friends. Just remember to keep it fairly brief, and the tone should be light and sound spontaneous, rather than contrived and over-rehearsed. Also, try not to pick a story that might embarrass the bride or groom.

speeches to avoid

The whole point of giving a wedding speech is to say something meaningful about the bride and groom and to present it to your audience in an entertaining way. But what are the things you *shouldn't* be saying as part of your wedding speech?

Anything too personal: This is not the time to be sharing family secrets or stories about ex-girlfriends/boyfriends/wives/husbands.

Anything too negative: Some light-hearted banter about the pitfalls of marriage is fine, but if you labor the point, people might start to think you really mean it.

Anything that involves "in"-jokes: If you think that half your audience won't understand the meaning behind any witty double-entendres you plan to put in your speech, leave them out.

Anything crude or on a sensitive subject: Graphic sex, religion, and politics have no place in your speech—you are bound to offend someone in the room.

Anything too short: Even if you are crippled with shyness, standing up and mumbling "Thanks" just isn't good enough.

Speech is an arrangement of notes that will never be played again.
Anonymous

Anything too long: You may think what you've written is hugely witty, but speak for much longer than ten minutes and you risk losing the attention of your audience.

Anything depressing: It is appropriate to mention absent friends and relatives, but keep the tone light. Going into lots of heart-rending detail about a dead mother/father/friend is not suitable for a wedding.

Anything too gushing: Don't get carried away using overly flowery language that will embarrass everyone, most of all you!

father of the bride

The bride's father is looked upon to offer thanks, congratulations, and, if nerves permit, a few words of wisdom on the subject of a successful marriage. He is not expected to give a long speech, but his will be the first speech of the day, so it's important that it sets the right tone.

If the father of the bride is deceased or cannot attend, the father of the groom or an older relative or friend should take his place.

The bride's father traditionally gets up to speak once the meal is over and the coffee has been served. He will be introduced by a toastmaster, if there is one; otherwise, he can get up at an agreed time to face his guests. It's always a good idea for the best man to give a "five-minute warning" that the speeches are about to begin, so all the guests are seated from the start … and stay seated until all the speakers have finished their speeches.

The father of the bride will normally start by welcoming everyone to the wedding and thanking the assembled guests for joining his family in celebrating the marriage of his daughter. He will then go on to remark on how beautiful his daughter looks and how proud he is feeling on such a special day. This is also an appropriate time to include a story or two about the groom joining the family and how lucky he is to be taking his daughter as his wife. A few words of advice about what it takes to enjoy a happy marriage are also appropriate— borrow from quotations, if necessary!

The father of the bride concludes his speech by asking the assembled guests to stand up as he proposes a toast to the bride and groom. At very formal American weddings, the father of the bride may also offer a simple toast to the flag. Whereas at British weddings, it's a toast to Her Majesty the Queen.

Love is a symbol of eternity.
It wipes out all sense of time,
destroying all memory of a beginning
and all fear of an end.

Anonymous

Simple speech for the father of the bride

Ladies and gentlemen. I would like to start by thanking you all for joining my wife and me on this very happy occasion as our daughter (name of bride) becomes (name of groom)'s wife. We are delighted to see that so many friends, old and new, have been able to make the journey to be with us—your company is an essential part of this wonderful day.

It is never easy for a father to see his daughter giving her heart to another man, but in this case I will have to make an exception. We have come to know (name of groom) very well over the past year and we are delighted to say that he is just the sort of man we had in mind as a son-in-law—kind, considerate, and hard-working—and I am sure he is going to make (name of bride) very happy. So, please stand up and raise your glasses and drink a toast to the health and happiness of (name of bride and groom).

the groom

The groom's speech is largely one of thanks and need not be very long. Three to five minutes is more than enough, but you do need to remember to thank the right people.

The groom speaks after the father of the bride and his first task is to offer thanks for his father-in-law's toast on behalf of himself and his new wife. He takes a moment to thank the assembled guests for coming to the wedding, perhaps mentioning specific people who have traveled some distance, and an overall comment on how much it means to have their friends and family in attendance. This is also a good time to comment about the quality of the reception, the wonderful meal and wine, and to thank both sets of parents for financial and emotional contributions and for making it all possible. It is also usual for the groom to present a bouquet of flowers to both mothers at this point as a thank you. If appropriate, the groom can also thank specific professionals involved in the organization of the wedding, like the chef, manager of the hall or a wedding organizer.

On pain of death, the groom must then say how beautiful his wife looks and that he cannot believe how lucky he is to have married such an amazing girl! You cannot be too slushy at this point; everyone will love you for it! Proposing a simple toast to your bride is also a good idea.

If there is an appropriate story about how the two of you met, the proposal, or asking her dad for her hand in marriage, this will come next. It may also be appropriate for the groom to mention recently deceased family or friends and how they are missed.

The groom's last big thank you goes to the bridesmaids. It is usual to refer to them by name and to call them up individually to receive a small gift. The groom proposes a toast to the bridesmaids, along the lines of "To our beautiful bridesmaids, your love and support on this special day has meant the world to us, thank you. The bridesmaids."

The groom then introduces his best man with a word or two about their relationship —and probably offering a warning that he keeps his speech appropriate … and clean!

Simple speech for the groom

Ladies and gentlemen. My wife and I would like to thank (name of parents) for their good wishes and join them in thanking you all for being with us today. Your company means so much to us both and as I look around the room I realize how lucky we are to have so many good friends who want to wish us well. I hope you all enjoyed the wonderful food and think you will agree that the chef has done a fantastic job. (Name of parents) also did a fantastic job helping us pay for it all, so a huge thank you to your check book as well!

What can I say about my beautiful bride? She looks more gorgeous today than I ever thought possible and she has made me the happiest man in the world by agreeing to become my wife. As someone once said, "Love puts the fun in together, the sad in apart, and the joy in a heart." Please raise your glasses to toast the beautiful bride; I love you with all my heart. The beautiful bride.

Moving swiftly on from all that slushy stuff, I remember the day (funny story/memory inserted here) …

And finally, it is my very great pleasure to honor our lovely bridesmaids. You all look stunning and have done such a brilliant job—not just today, but in the last few weeks, when (name of bride) was close to turning into Bridezilla, you kept her more hysterical moments in check, and for that I thank you. To show our appreciation we have bought each of you a little gift which I would be delighted if you would come up to receive (list name of each bridesmaid). And now I would ask that everyone stand up as I toast our beautiful bridesmaids. The bridesmaids.

I love thee to the depth and breadth and height
My soul can reach.
Elizabeth Barrett Browning (1806–1861)

the best man

If you've been asked to be a best man at a wedding, your instant reaction is probably to say "Not likely!" But don't be too quick to dismiss what is, after all, quite an honor. Someone out there thinks enough of you to want you to speak on their behalf on what is probably the most important day of their life.

Of all the words said at a wedding, the ones that are anticipated most are those uttered by the best man. Rightly or wrongly, there's huge pressure to entertain with a performance filled with clever anecdotes, witty stories, and the odd moment that will bring a tear to the eye. It's little wonder most men dread being asked.

Don't let nerves be a reason for turning the task down. Providing you do some research so you feel prepared, and then rehearse until you are practically word perfect, your performance should go without a hitch.

The best man's speech traditionally comes last after the groom, and the bride if she is saying a few words. He needs to start by thanking the groom on behalf of the bridesmaids for his kind words and adding his own thoughts on how gorgeous they all look. He should also say how beautiful the bride is and what a lucky man the groom is to have won over the affections of such a lovely wife.

It is then appropriate to say something about his relationship with the groom and how long they have known one another, which should lead nicely on to a story or two about adolescent exploits. If telling jokes is not your forte, don't feel you have to tell any. A poorly delivered joke is definitely worse than none at all. Finally, since the best man's speech rounds off the formal part of the reception, it is up to him to propose the final toast to the bride and groom.

Simple speech for the best man

Thank you (name of groom) for those kind words and thank you on behalf of our lovely bridesmaids—they were obviously chosen for their stunning good looks as well as their ability to walk in a straight line up the aisle. And, while on the subject of beauty, I feel I have to add my own words of wonder for our beautiful bride. Doesn't she look gorgeous? (Name of groom) is a very lucky man—it's a good thing that I didn't meet her first, because then it would be me getting married today and he would be making this embarrassing speech!

I have known (name of groom) since we were at elementary school together and we have enjoyed each other's company pretty much ever since. And I think the time has come for you to learn a thing or two about this fine young man. (Insert story or two reminiscing about high school/college/sporting highs and lows.)

He first met (name of bride) at (name of location), and to say it was love at first sight is an understatement. This handsome, self-assured creature you see before you was reduced to a gibbering wreck. But making a decision has never been his strong point and it still took two months of drooling before he finally asked her out … and the rest, of course, is history. And don't they make a lovely couple?

Today has been a truly memorable and hugely enjoyable occasion, I think you will all agree. The perfect place with perfect food and perfect wine for a perfect couple. So please stand up and top off your glasses and join me in toasting the bride and groom. May all your problems be little ones. The bride and groom.

At some weddings, the best man will also read out messages from a selection of cards given to the bride and groom, as well as any telegrams of good wishes that have been sent from absent friends or relatives. This adds a nice touch, especially if the messages add a bit of humor to the occasion. After proposing the final toast, it's then the best man's duty to announce that the formal part of the wedding is over and that the bride and groom are about to cut the cake. This is also a good point to mention any other times, like the start of the dancing, when a supper buffet will be served, and also an indication of when the evening is likely to end, so that guests can make arrangements to get back to their home or hotel.

the bride

The bride giving a speech at her own wedding is a fairly recent innovation, but it is becoming increasingly popular as she becomes more involved in every aspect of the planning and paying for the big day.

Whether or not you make a speech is entirely up to you. Traditionally the groom speaks on behalf of both himself and his bride, but if you feel you want to add your own words of thanks or perhaps say something meaningful to your groom in front of your guests, then go for it!

There is no formal requirement for what the bride has to say, but it makes most sense for her to get up just after the groom and before the best man. You may like to start by adding your own thanks to everyone for coming to the wedding and to both sets of parents for financial and emotional support.

Saying a few loving words to your groom will go down well with your audience, especially if you have kept your speech as a surprise from everyone. Tell him how delighted you are to have become his wife and how you are looking forward to a long and happy life together. You can add a little anecdote or two about your relationship (great, if it's a little embarrassing) at the same time. And many modern brides have been known to break into verse or even a song at this point to express their feelings.

I dreamed of a wedding of elaborate elegance,
A church filled with family and friends.
I asked him what kind of wedding he wished for,
He said one that would make me his wife.
Anonymous

Simple speech for the bride

Ladies and gentleman, before we get to the best man's speech I hope you will indulge me as I say a few words. My getting up to speak has come as something of a shock to (name of groom), as you can probably tell by the expression on his face. But I just cannot let this moment pass without telling you (name of groom) how much I love you in front of our family and friends. It goes without saying that you are the luckiest man in the world to have married me. And I am the luckiest girl for marrying you. I know we are going to be very happy together and I can't wait to start the adventure that is marriage with you by my side. So everyone please join me in offering a toast to my wonderful groom. "May we love as long as we live, and live as long as we love." The groom.

the maid of honor and parents of the groom

At a modern wedding it is becoming more popular for people other than traditional speakers to get up and say a few words or tell a short story about the bride and/or groom that will entertain the guests. These should be thought of as extended toasts rather than full-blown speeches, and you should always get the agreement of the bride and groom in advance before jumping up to speak.

Speeches and toasts are a lovely part of any wedding but you don't want to overdo it by having too many people stepping up to the microphone. It's all a question of balance. If it is known that the father of the bride is not a natural performer and will be keeping it brief, this obviously allows time for a gregarious father of the groom to take his turn in the spotlight.

The maid of honor

The maid of honor can get up and say a few words just before the best man makes his speech, offering a different perspective on the bride and the groom. She may also like to tell a short story about the bride, her wedding obsession, and give a little insight into how she felt when she met the groom. The overall tone should be light and humorous. She may also like to propose a toast to the bride, the bride and groom, or the best man and ushers.

The father/parents of the groom

The groom's parents can get somewhat sidelined at a wedding but they have an equally important role to play, especially as these days they are just as likely to have made a financial contribution as the bride's parents. The father of the groom can speak just after the bride and groom, thanking them for their kind words. He may also like to add a little story about the groom, as well as personal good wishes for a long and happy married life.

TOASTS

wedding toasts

A traditional wedding usually features a combination of both speeches and toasts, but what exactly is a toast? The simple answer is that it's an expression of thanks, love, and affection offered to the bride and groom by their friends and family, and also by the bride and groom to their guests.

A toast is usually quite short and traditionally only a line or two of good wishes, although these days the speaker may make it more personal by adding a short anecdote about the recipient. It is also appropriate to draw from famous or funny quotations to enhance a toast or to lead into a story of your own.

Traditional toasts are made by the following members of the bridal party:

- **Father of the bride** toasts the bride and groom (and often the assembled guests as a thank you for coming).

- **The groom** toasts the bridesmaids (and his bride if he is feeling romantic).

- **The bride** toasts her groom.

- **The best man** toasts the bride and groom (and any absent friends).

It is usual for the recipient of a toast to "reply" offering their thanks, so the groom thanks the father of the bride, and the best man thanks the groom on behalf of the bridesmaids. If the bride and groom are the recipients of many toasts during the reception, it is acceptable for them to simply raise their glasses in acknowlededgment, rather than to keep saying thank you! Once a toast is proposed, it is expected that the guests stand up and raise their glasses, taking a sip of their drink, which serves as agreement for what the speaker has said. The recipient remains seated as they accept the toast.

TOASTS TO THE BRIDE
AND GROOM

I wish you health; I wish you wealth;
I wish you gold in store;
I wish you heaven when you die,
What could I wish you more?

Here's to the groom with bride so fair.
And here's to the bride with groom so rare!

Here's to the bride and groom.
May their happiness last forever and
may we be fortunate enough to continue
being a part of it.

May you have many children
And may they grow mature in taste
And healthy in color
And as sought after
As the contents of this glass.
Traditional Irish toast

A toast to love and laughter,
And happily ever after.

May the best day of your past be the
worst day of your future.

May you have warm words on a cold
evening, a full moon on a dark night, and a
smooth road all the way to your door.
Traditional Irish toast

A toast to sweethearts. May all sweethearts
become married couples, and may all
married couples remain sweethearts.

Here's to the new husband
And here's to the new wife
May they remain lovers
For all of their life.
Traditional toast

Love one another and be happy. It's as simple
and as difficult as that.

My greatest wish for the two of you is that
through the years your love for each other will
deepen and grow, that years from now you
will look back on this day as the day
you loved each other the least.
Traditional toast

May for "better or worse" be far better
than worse.

May your love be as endless as your
wedding rings.

Never marry for money,
you can borrow it cheaper.
Scottish Proverb

Shared joy is a double joy;
shared sorrow is half a sorrow.
Swedish Proverb

TOASTS MADE BY
THE FATHER OF THE BRIDE

*It is written that when children find true
love, parents find true joy.
Here's to your joy and ours, from this day
and forever more.*

*Here are some wise words to live by:
"Love to one, friendship to many,
and goodwill to all."*

*Wise words for the groom:
The most effective way of remembering your
wedding anniversary is to forget
it once.*

*Wise words for the groom:
Here's to the lasses we've loved, my lad
Here's to the lips we've pressed;
For of kisses and lasses
Like liquor in glasses,
The last is always the best.*
Traditional Scottish toast

TOASTS FROM THE BRIDE
TO HER GROOM

I love you more than yesterday and less than
I will tomorrow.

May we love as long as we live,
And live as long as we love.

I have spread my dreams under your feet;
Tread softly because you tread on my dreams.
W. B. Yeats (1865–1939)

Love me, sweet with all thou art,
Feeling, thinking, seeing;
Love me in the lightest part,
Love me in full being.
Elizabeth Barrett Browning (1806–1861)

Here's to the man that's good and sweet,
Here's to the man that's true.
Here's to the man that rules my heart,
In other words, here's to you.
Traditional toast

TOASTS FROM THE GROOM
TO HIS BRIDE

I have known many, liked not a few.
Loved only one, I toast to you.

To my bride. She knows all about me and
loves me just the same.

Grow old along with me.
The best is yet to be.
Robert Browning (1812–1889)

When the heart is full,
the tongue cannot speak.
Scottish proverb

Because I love you truly,
Because you love me, too,
My greatest happiness
Is sharing life with you.
Traditional toast

TOASTS BY THE BEST MAN

Here's a toast to your new bride, who has everything a girl could want in her life, except for good taste in men!

May your hands be forever clasped in friendship And your hearts joined forever in love.

*A health to you,
A wealth to you,
And the best that life can give to you.
May fortune still be kind to you.
And happiness be true to you.
And life be long and good to you.
This is a toast of all your friends to you.*
Traditional Irish toast

*May you be poor in misfortunes and rich in blessings,
Slow to make enemies and quick to make friends,
And may you know nothing but happiness from this day forward.*
Traditional Irish toast

Here's to the bride. May your hours of joy be as numerous as the petals on your bouquet.

Here's to the groom, a man who keeps his head though loses his heart.

TOASTS TO THE BRIDESMAIDS

*"A thing of beauty is a joy forever."
Here's to these beautiful bridesmaids.*
John Keats (1795–1821)

"I have half a dozen healths to drink to these fair ladies."
William Shakespeare, *Henry VIII*

TOASTS TO THE ASSEMBLED GUESTS

Let us toast the bride;
Let us toast the groom;
Let us toast the person that tied;
Let us toast every guest in the room.
Traditional toast

"I drink to the general joy of the whole table."
William Shakespeare, *Macbeth*

May the friends of our youth be the
companions of our old age.

Here's to eternity—may we spend it in as
good company as this night finds us.

It is around the table that friends
understand best the warmth of being together.
Italian proverb

TOASTS TO THE PARENTS

God could not be everywhere
so he made mothers.
Proverb

A father is someone you look up to
no matter how tall they grow.
Proverb

TOAST TO GRANDPARENTS

Let us raise our glasses
And then imbibe
To the splendid couple
Who founded this tribe.
Traditional toast

TOAST TO ABSENT FRIENDS

Absent friends—though out of sight we
recognize them with our glasses.

... and finally

All these phrases translate to
"your health" and could be
used at the end of any toast.
Cheers! (English)
A votre santé! (French)
Cin Cin! (Italian)
Salud! (Spanish)
Prost! (German)
Mazel tov! (Jewish)
Chai yo! (Thai)
Skal! (Scandinavian)

Champagne is the classic toasting
drink, but you can look to other
cultures for originality.

Beer (Germany, Austria, Belgium)
Wine (Greece, Italy, Portugal)
Vodka (Russia, Poland)
Rum (Jamaica, Bahamas, Cuba)
Whisky (Scotland, Ireland)
Sake (Japan)
Tequila (Mexico)

Useful Web site addresses

Speech Writers and Courses

Fine Speeches
www.finespeeches.com

Skills Studio
www.skillstudio.co.uk

Sparkling Speeches
www.sparklingspeeches.co.uk

Utter Wit
www.utterwit.co.uk

Wedding Speech Builder
www.weddingspeechbuilder.com

Write 4 Me
www.writeforme.co.uk

Web sites for inspiration and quotes

www.quotegarden.com

www.coolquotes.com

www.innocentenglish.com

www.presentationhelper.co.uk

www.freeweddingspeech.com

www.matrimonialbank.com/jokes/html

www.theknot.com/

Picture Credits

Key: ph= photographer, a=above, b=below, r=right, l=left, c=center.

Polly Wreford pages 1, 3 both, 4-5, 7ar, 8-9, 13, 14, 15, 17a, 20, 21b, 22-23, 24, 28, 30l, 30 all, 31, 35, 37, 41br, 42, 44, 45, 53, 54, 54-55, 57, 58, 59, 62, 63

Caroline Arber: pages 12, 17c, 32, 34, 36, 36-37, 41cr, 43, 49r

Dan Duchars pages 2, 7cr, 7br, 16 inset, 17b, 46-47, 48

Peter Cassidy pages 10-11, 50-51, 60-61, 64

David Loftus pages 21a, 25, 27

Viv Yeo pages 19 inset, 41ar, 49l

Carolyn Barber pages 10 inset, 56

Craig Fordham pages 39, 61 inset

Debi Treloar pages 18, 19 background

Ian Wallace pages 7l, 52

Alan Williams pages 26, 41l

William Lingwood page 16-17 background